Chemical-Free Cleaning: The Best 100 DIY Recipes for Natural Home Cleaning

Click Here To Receive Free Kindle Books To Your Email Daily

Promo Kindle
Knowledge is better when it's free

www.PromoKindle.com

All rights Reserved. No part of this publication or the information in it may be quoted from or reproduced in any form by means such as printing, scanning, photocopying or otherwise without prior written permission of the copyright holder.

Disclaimer and Terms of Use: Effort has been made to ensure that the information in this book is accurate and complete, however, the author and the publisher do not warrant the accuracy of the information, text and graphics contained within the book due to the rapidly changing nature of science, research, known and unknown facts and Internet. The Author and the publisher do not hold any responsibility for errors, omissions or contrary interpretation of the subject matter herein. This book is presented solely for motivational and informational purposes only.

Table of Contents

Intro: Explaining the Benefits of Natural Home Cleaners 5

Recipes for the Kitchen 9

Recipes for the Bathroom 14

Laundry Recipes 18

Recipes for Bedrooms 23

Recipes for Living Spaces 26

Recipes for Floors 31

Recipes for Playrooms 34

Recipes for the Garden 38

Recipes for the Garage and Car 42

Recipes for Outdoor Spaces 45

Conclusion 48

References 49

Intro: Explaining the Benefits of Natural Home Cleaners

Whether you are starting a new go green initiative, or you only use organic and do it yourself recipes and ingredients at home, by using these top tips for recipes to help you create *Do It Yourself* cleaning products around the house, you can find that not only are you using natural products, but you're helping to save the environment and promote healthy breathing and looking out for you and your family!

NATURAL IS BETTER

Maybe you grew up with the certain products in your house that your mom or grandmother would always use, but no one really knew about the harmful side effects of these products. Maybe all they focused on was that everything smelled clean and fresh!

Smelling clean and being healthy for the environment and for our bodies are two different things. If you pick up any bottle of cleanser or even aerosol sprays that are supposed to make the environment smell nice, if you read the ingredients, usually one of the first warnings that you might see are that it reads "Don't inhale" or "Toxic."

That's why we've put together natural recipes for you that you can make at home. You'll find great recipes for your kitchen, bathroom, bedroom, floors, playroom, outdoor spaces, garden, garage and more! Be sure to utilize these fresh tips as you find do it yourself recipes to help you go organic and stay green. Maybe you're not aware of this, but a lot of cleaning products that our families grew up with are no longer being used. It was found over the years that some of these products are not safe and can be very harmful and very toxic if inhaled; or if they are left out in areas near heat, they can get hot and the cans can leak harmful toxins or explode. Sometimes we store things like oven cleaner in an area in the kitchen where it can be against pipes that are hot or warm, or near an oven that can get very hot.

NEW WAYS TO REPLACE OLD PRODUCTS

Learn from these tips a few new ideas for cleaning spaces, ways to help to keep rooms brightened and fresh, or put together a few natural cleaning products and give them to family and friends to use. Either way, gone are the days of having your house smell like Pine-Sol and Lysol, and they are being replaced with natural remedies and natural herbal products that can help promote, create and contribute to clean living and sustainability for our environment. Why would you want to buy a product that smells like lemon when you can use real lemons?

WHY WE SHOULD AVOID HARMFUL CLEANSERS

When we utilize products like certain cleansers that are very harmful and toxic to the skin, they clearly have warning labels that read that we should not inhale the fumes from these products, and yet every day, we find after cleaning out the tub or cleaning the sink, that we are breathing in that sweet smell that they scent these products with. Maybe its lavender, maybe its lemon, or maybe it's what they consider a fresh scent, but what ends up happening over time is that we are inhaling toxic fumes and then we start coughing because we realize, "Oh I just inhaled too much." That's not the problem!

The problem is that were inhaling fumes from toxic chemicals that are not meant to be breathed in. We then leave them for a long period under the cabinet, and this might be something that was recalled—like Scrubbing Bubbles! Additionally, if you look at any household cleaner and you turn it over and look at the back and read the warning label, it may read that there's a hazard to breathing in the fumes, or you may find that it says you can only use it when you wear gloves.

Some people who use Drano, for example, don't even know and are not even aware that the product is so harmful that they recommend that you wear gloves when you use it. They also recommend you stand a good distance back when you're pouring it down your drain and lean back as far as you can away from the sink because if the product splashes on you or gets on you, it can be very harmful and cause skin irritations, rashes, and even cause blindness if it gets into your eyes.

DON'T GO BY THE CARTOON CHARACTERS—THESE ARE HARMFUL PRODUCTS

These are products that we use every day, and we see these commercials where they show these cartoon characters selling these products, and we are exposing our children to these items. That's why we put together a few great do it yourself the recipes that can help to ensure that as you go green, and as you learn to create your own cleansing products and different sprays for your rooms, you'll find that not only will this help you to make your home a more natural environment, but that it's cleaner, safer, and you don't have to worry about toxic fumes that can cause things like various types of cancers.

As you go through the recipes, you'll quickly find that you already have the ingredients, well most of them, in your cabinet and these usually include things like vinegar, baking soda and other products that you typically have at home. And even if you don't have products like eucalyptus oil, you will find that as soon as you go out and buy these and start making your products, that not only will you feel safer, but these are actually products you can touch and breathe in as they are not harmful to you.

That's why we want you to enjoy the recipes, explore them, and don't be afraid to experiment with changing the scents and the smells for the various types of cleaning products that you're going to make so that way you can ensure that you are using homeopathic ingredients, natural ingredients and you're also working to save the environment and to stay healthy!

RECIPES FOR ALL YOUR NEEDS

Recipes for do it yourself, natural home cleaners include recipes for the kitchen, the bathroom, laundry, bedrooms, living spaces, floors, playrooms, garden, garage and car. With these 100 recipes, we hope that you'll find a few that maybe you haven't even heard of or used before that you can pass on to your friends and family to help our environment and to keep your home natural and safe! So let's begin!

Recipes for the Kitchen

To start with, in your do it yourself recipes, there are a few key ingredients that you're going to need and you can find these in your kitchen on the shelf, in a refrigerator or at your local store!

BASIC INGREDIENTS

For starters, make sure that you have baking soda, hydrogen peroxide, white vinegar, borax if needed, olive oil or vegetable oil, and citrus fruits like lemons, limes or even oranges, as this will lend fragrance to your various cleaning products. There are essential oils that you can order online if you want, including tea tree oil, lavender oil, lemongrass, eucalyptus and even rose-scented oil. You will also need water.

TOOLS

You may want to find a small spatula that you can use as well as a spray bottle or various sized spray bottles that you can leave your cleaning products in once you've made them. You will also need measuring spoons, paper towels, a mixing bowl, and scrubbing sponges.

Normally, when you clean your kitchen counter and other spaces, you would have your dish detergent, and you would also have some type of cleaner like a multi purpose spray to wipe your oven, fridge, floors, and counters.

1. All-Purpose Cleaner

    In a mixing bowl, add 1 teaspoon of baking soda, about 2 tablespoons of vinegar,
    and 1 half teaspoon of dish soap, if you use a version like Meyer's natural dish detergent. You can mix your ingredients in a mixing bowl, and then add it to a spray bottle. Next, fill the bottle the rest of the way with water and then shake it up.

2. Lavender Scented All-Purpose Cleaner

    To make this version, you would mix the all-purpose cleaner in the same manner that you did, but this time add a few drops of lavender essential oil after you've made the ingredients and put everything in the mixing bottle. Use a few drops of the lavender essential oil and add it directly into the spray bottle. You can shake it up and then test it out in the sink, for example, to see how you like the smell of it and if you need to add a few more drops of lavender, you can do that. If you want to utilize this cleaner in different cabinets, on surfaces, on the refrigerator, it will work well because it's a very clean scent.

3. Lemon Scented All Purpose Cleaner

    You can make lemon scented cleaner using the same all-purpose cleaner recipe that you started with, but this time use lemon essence oil and you can also try to mix in a little lemon tea tree oil. The benefit to adding this to your recipe will be that you have a cleaning product that is very similar to the product that you were using before, but this is an all-natural remedy that's going to be healthy for your home.

4. Scrubbing Cleaner For Your Kitchen

   To make a cleaner for your kitchen that you can also use when you're cleaning dishes, on the countertop and even around the stove area where you get food that might be grimy and dried up, in a mixing bowl, put in a third cup of baking soda and then add in water—just enough to make it moist and doughy. It should be a little thick like tooth paste. Once you mix it together, you can use a sponge that has the bristle end to help you to be able to scrub the surfaces and various areas that you want to clean. You can store this and use it, or you can make it fresh each time.

5. Garbage Disposal Cleaner

   One of the easiest ways to clean your garbage disposal is to take a lemon and actually cut it into a few pieces and put it into the disposal and turn the disposal on. As you run the water, let the disposal grind up the lemon and this will help to give it a fresh clean scent.

6. Grease Remover for Stove Tops

   In order to clean grease off of the stove top, a very simple process is available and all you need to do is use vinegar. You can use undiluted vinegar and just put it into one of your spray bottles and mark it as undiluted vinegar for your stove top so that way, you know exactly what it is. Keep in mind that as you add to your recipes, you're going to want to label your bottles. Spray your stove with your vinegar, being careful not to go near the burners. Let the mixture rest for a few minutes, and then wipe it with a cloth. The vinegar will help to break down any dried food that is on the stove.

7. Cleaning Your Stove Top with Baking Soda

    Another option for cleaning up grease and residue is you can use baking soda that you apply to a damp cloth, or you can use a sponge that has a bristle end. Simply add a little baking soda but not so much that you're creating a cloud and just rub it in with your sponge to get the grease off. You can clean this up with a damp cloth.

8. Removing Grime from Stove Tops

    If you're finding that you see grime on your stove top counter, you can actually boil water in a small pot and pour a little hot water on the stove. Let it sit in a tiny little puddle and that way it helps to loosen up the dried food or grease that's there, and then you can gently wipe it off. You can use baking soda as a scrubber to wipe it down for any tough spots.

9. Another Recipe for Cleaning the Stove Top

    Try using your vinegar and warm soapy water where the grime builds up. You can add your vinegar and let it rest for about 15 minutes, then take it off and you should be able to scrub down the areas.

10. How to clean the oven naturally

    The simplest and easiest way to clean your oven is when it is turned off. Sprinkle a little baking soda on to the bottom of the oven. You want it to be completely coated. Try not to get baking soda on the wires but if you do, you can wipe that off. Then your next step is to take warm water and vinegar that you put into a spray bottle and spray it vigorously around the area so that is completely saturated. You don't want it soaking wet and dripping onto the floor but just enough to cover the baking soda.

You will start to see it foam up a little bit and that's the whole idea. Let it sit for about 30 minutes. Once you come back to it, you can take the scrub brush side of your dish sponge and this is going to be safe for you to clean your oven. Don't use a really harsh scrubbing pad because you don't want to strip the paint, but you can use a scrub brush like a Brillo pad or copper wire brush because these are usually used for kitchen purposes. Use a damp cloth to wipe down any residue.

Recipes for the Bathroom

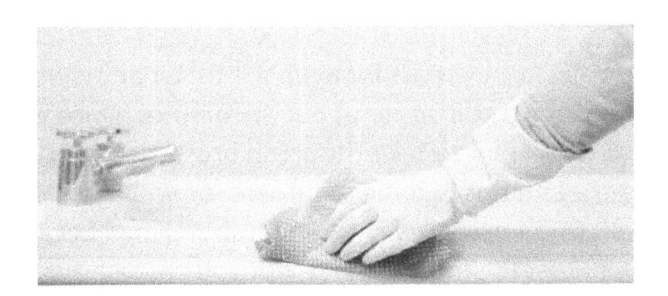

When it comes to keeping your bathroom clean, while you think it might be difficult to find green recipes, we have a few key ingredients that you're going to find right in your cabinet!

For your bathroom you will need baking soda, you can use castile soap, vegetable oil, liquid soap, distilled white vinegar and salt. If you have kosher salt, that's good. You're also going to need water, so maybe you want to just use tap water for this part.

Equipment that you are going to need includes your measuring cups, measuring spoons that you want to use, your empty spray bottles and labels are so that you can mark down what you have made. You will also need a small bowl and a mixing spoon so that you have something to make your ingredients with.

11. Scrubbing Powder

Mix together a cup of baking soda and add in a cup of salt. You can use kosher salt if you have it. What you're going to do is sprinkle this in your tub, and this is going to serve as your cleanser. You can add a tiny bit of water to it if you want. What this represents is the old type of Comet that we used to use that was in a powder form to clean out the tub but try not to inhale it as it might make you sneeze!

12. Tile Cleanser

In a small bowl, mix together about a cup of baking soda with ½ cup of vegetable oil based liquid soap mixture, then add in ½ cup of water; you can add 1 to 2 tablespoons of vinegar to your mixture and stir together. Next, you can pour it into a spray bottle and put the lid on and label it. You can use this to clean off your tiles, the counters, and you can even clean the tub with this. This should last you for a little while, and if you are worried that you're going to lose your recipe, you can always write it on the side of the label so you know the ingredients!

13. Drain Cleaner

Mix together in a bowl ½ cup of baking soda and then add in 1 cup of vinegar. For this recipe, you can pour it in the drain slowly and let it rest. You can then rinse it with hot water and let it wash through, but you may need to repeat the recipe or do it overnight and let it sit until the morning.

14. Toilet Cleaner

In a cup, mix together ½ cup of baking soda and a cup of vinegar. You can add this into your toilet and let it sit. Use your scrub brush and then clean any debris that's in the toilet and flush it. Make sure to mix this over the toilet or sink. It might foam up!

15. Glass and Window Cleaner

You can use a large spray bottle for this as it will be something that can last for a while. Take 4 cups of warm water, and combine it with ¼ cup of vinegar. You can mix together gently and use it to clean your mirrors, glass, and windows. An old recipe used newspaper to wipe windows down with this. A dry cloth or paper towel can suffice.

16. Floor Cleaner

Take 2 gallons of hot water and add ½ cup of baking soda to it. You can apply this with a mop and rinse as needed.

17. Grime Remover

Similar to the oven recipe, sprinkle baking soda into your grimy areas such as the tile, floors or in the tub, and you can spray vinegar or you can add salt and use a scrub brush and gently get out all of the debris dirt and grime.

18. Mildew Remover

Mix together ½ cup of baking soda and ½ cup of vinegar. Make sure that it becomes thick like toothpaste, and you can use this to scrub different areas in the bathroom around sinks, counters, the base of the toilet and even the tank.

19. Disinfecting Spray

Make one bottle with hydrogen peroxide and a spray nozzle for it and then make a separate bottle that is straight vinegar and water. For the vinegar and water, use equal amounts of vinegar and water. Spray one bottle, then spray the other one on the surface and wait about a minute or two and wipe down any residue. This will kill any bacteria that are on surfaces, walls, and floors. DO NOT MIX THE TWO INGREDIENTS TOGETHER, THOUGH. THIS CAN CAUSE A

BAD CHEMICAL REACTION. DO NOT MIX THEM IN THE SAME BOTTLE!

20. Bathroom Cleaner

Mix together 1 cup of vinegar that is slightly warm. You can heat it briefly in the microwave, but it should not be hot, just slightly warm, and then add dish detergent to it. Use about 1 cup. When you mix it together, you can actually put this into a spray bottle and use it for tiles, cabinets, floors and other surfaces around the bathroom.

Laundry Recipes

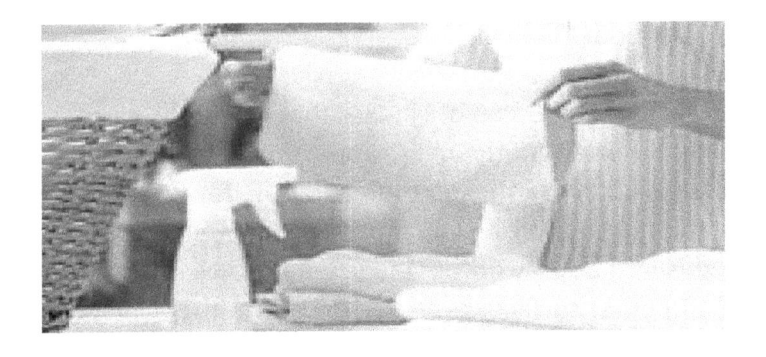

As it relates to laundry detergent and different types of cleaners for your clothing, there are a few different types of recipes that you can use and some will require ingredients like soap, borax and even washing soda. We put together a few top recipes that can help you get started; just make sure to follow them closely and look for things along the way that can help you to minimize the time it takes to make them. You can always double up a recipe or cut it in half.

The types of ingredients that you will need include essential oils, borax, Dr. Bronner's soap, washing soda and the equipment that you will use may include a blender or food processor, a grater, mixing cups, a pot, a large gallon size container with a lid, spoons, mixing bowls and labels to ensure that you label everything properly.

21. Laundry Detergent

   You will need a bar of Dr. Bronner's soap, and it can be lavender, citrus, almond, or even peppermint if you want to scent it, one cup of borax, one cup of Arm & Hammer washing soda and possibly a few drops of tea tree essential oil to help disinfect clothes. In a saucepan or mixing bowl, you can grate the soap. Next, add it to a pot with two cups of water and soak it. You will see it start to dissolve in the water.

Use a five gallon bucket or something that's really large and industrial size, and keep in mind it is going to be heavy when you fill it, add the borax, the tea tree if you're going to use it and the washing soda. As you start to mix it, you may see it separate right away as you add water to it. You are going to fill it about ¾ of the way and then put a lid on top of that and close it up. Let it rest overnight and then in the morning, you can use about ½ cup to a cup for each wash that you're going to use.

22. Another Version of Laundry Detergent

Ingredients include 1/2 bar soap that you grate down and a half cup of borax and ½ cup of washing soda. Boil 2 cups of water in a pan and add the soap in slowly. Let it dissolve, but you don't want it to be completely melted, so take it off the fire once it starts to melt. Then add it to a large container once it is dissolved, and you can fill this up with water.

Add in the washing soda and add the borax. Try not to get any lumps. Make sure that when you add the water, you check for lumps and get any clumps out of it. Let it sit for about 24 hours. You can check back to make sure you get any additional clumps out of it. What will happen after 24 hours is that it will become a gel-like substance and when you see that, that's when it's ready for you to use. You can use ¼ to ½ cup for loads and ½ cup with loads that are really heavily-soiled clothes. Keep in mind it may foam or bubble up in the washing machine the more that you add to it.

23. Rinse to Clean Out Your Washing Machine

Let your washing machine fill up with hot water and set it on the largest setting possible setting for a large load. Let the water fill up but don't add any clothes or anything else to it and then fill it with three to four cups of white vinegar. Let it run on that particular cycle, and this will help to ensure that your washing machine rinses itself thoroughly. Once the water has filled up, you can add ½ cup of baking soda. Let the water sit in the mixture for about 30 minutes to an hour to ensure that it's able to get rid of some of the gunk that builds up in the washing machine over time.

You can use a damp cloth and gloves if you'd like to rinse the inside of the washing machine while the water is in it. Keep in mind that this is hot water, so you may want to put gloves on and don't scald yourself. If you have a small scrub brush, you can use that to get around the areas where you see dried residue from old laundry detergent or you can even use a tooth brush to get into the little crevices.

24. Laundry Detergent in a Powdered Form

6 cups of borax, 4 cups of baking soda, 4 cups of washing soda (Arm and Hammer is fine), 4 cups of bar soap (grated/shredded). Mix everything together gently and store it in a large, sealed container.

You can use a $1/8^{th}$ cup of the mixture for your laundry for each load.

25. Laundry Detergent Powdered (has to be mixed)

Combine ¼ cup of liquid castile soap, 1 cup of washing soda, 1 cup of baking soda and 1 cup of white vinegar. Mix all the ingredients together and they should be stored in a container with a secure lid. The mix will be thick but over time it will dry out.

You can use ¼ cup to ½ cup for each load.

26. Lemon or Eucalyptus Scented Fabric Softener

    White vinegar and several drops of scented lemon or eucalyptus essential oil. You can add ¼ to ½ cup of the vinegar to the rinse cycle and add a few drops of the oil before you add it.

27. Lavender or Mint Scented Fabric Softener

    Use the vinegar method from #26 and add lavender essential oil or mint.

28. Eucalyptus Scented Cleaning Spray

    In this recipe, mix together 2 tablespoons of vinegar, 1 teaspoon of baking soda and ½ teaspoon of dish soap. Mix your ingredients together in a mixing bowl and then spoon or pour it into an empty spray bottle. Fill the bottle with water and shake it up. Next, add a few drops of Eucalyptus essential oil to scent.

29. Lemon Scented Cleaning Spray

    Use the recipe above, and substitute the eucalyptus oil with lemon and tea tree or green tea oil. The benefit is that it will give your laundry room a fresh scent without the toxins from aerosol sprays!

30. Fabric Softener Using Socks

    For a quick fabric softener, you can soak a sock in vinegar and throw it in the washing machine with a load of clothes. The vinegar will help to spruce up the towels. Another tip to use is to put a few drops of your favorite essential oil on a sock and put that in the dryer. It won't stain the clothes, and they will smell heavenly or like vanilla!

Recipes for Bedrooms

To start cleaning your bedroom, these are a few great recipes to help ensure that everything is clean, neat and tidy without having to rely on aerosol sprays and toxic fumes to clean. Try these out, and you'll find they are all natural and safe.

31. Wood Furniture Cleaner

    You will need a lemon, a dry cloth, a small container with a lid, 1 tablespoon of water and 1 tablespoon of flax oil, olive oil or mineral oil. Mix the juice of the lemon with the oil and the water. Add this to your container and you can dip your cloth in it to wipe down wood furniture.

32. Wood Floor Cleaner

    Use the aforementioned recipe and instead of adding the mix to a container, add it to a gallon jug and fill it with warm water. You can mop your floors with this, and it will leave a fresh scent!

33. Lavender Scented Sheets

    You can use a few drops of lavender essential oil in a spray bottle with water. Shake it up and spray your sheets with it lightly a few hours before bedtime.

34. Eucalyptus Scented Curtains

    Everyone likes a room that smells fresh. Use a spray bottle filled with water and add a few drops of eucalyptus essential oil to it. Shake it up and lightly spray your curtains and drapes.

35. Natural Buffer for Your Nightstand or Desk

    If you have scratches in your wood night stand or desk, use a walnut that you crack in half and rub the inside of the nut on the wood.

36. Bedroom Furniture Polish

    You can use beeswax that you wipe on with a dry cloth and this can help to keep your furniture looking fresh! It won't break down over time and also works on cutting boards in the kitchen.

37. Carpet Cleaner

    If you have stubborn stains in your bedroom carpet, mix together ¼ cup of vinegar, ¼ cup borax and ¼ cup of salt. You can rub this into the rug and allow it to sit for a few hours. It will dry and then you can just vacuum up any residue.

38. Bedroom Window Cleaner

    A tiny bit of vinegar added to a spray bottle can clean bedroom windows fast. You can also wipe down mirrors, the front of the TV and other glass, but don't use newspaper, which can sometimes scratch TV screens. Use a cloth and wipe lightly!

39. Fresh Comforters

Use 2 tablespoons of white vinegar, 2 tablespoons of fabric softener and mix the ingredients together in a spray bottle. Fill it with water, and you can then add vanilla extract for a fresh aroma to your comforters.

40. Clean and Fresh Scented Clothing Drawers

Use the above recipe, but substitute the vanilla extract for eucalyptus essential oil and thoroughly saturate a sachet pillow. Let it air dry, then leave it in the drawer with clothes that you want to smell fresh. You can also use this recipe and substitute the eucalyptus for lavender and leave it under bed pillows for a great night's sleep!

Recipes for Living Spaces

Because your living spaces might include you, the whole family, kids, the dogs, cat, neighbors, and friends, we know this is a high-traffic area that you want to keep clean. Use these recipes to help you freshen up the green way!

For these recipes you will need essential oils, beeswax, water, vinegar, and fabric softener. Your tools will be spray bottles, dry cloths and measuring spoons.

41. Living Room Coffee Table Polish

    Try a little beeswax on wood tables with a dry cloth to wipe them down. It won't leave a stain or a mess and you can see the real wood shine through!

42. Fresh Carpet

    If you want to spruce up your living room carpet, instead of sprinkling a powder you buy, make your own with a little essential oil and water in a spray bottle. Eucalyptus is a nice scent, or you can go with lemon and it won't stain your carpet. Once you run the vacuum cleaner, the aroma will linger in the air!

43. Living Room Window Cleaner

Add a little vinegar in a spray bottle filled with water, and you can quickly clean your windows. There are no harsh fumes, and the vinegar smell will dissipate fast! You can also wipe off any mirrors or a coffee table if it is glass.

44. Fresh Living Room Pillows and Cushions

Add about 2 tablespoons of vinegar, 2 tablespoons of lavender, fresh scent or mountain-scented fabric softener and combine the ingredients together in a spray bottle. Fill the bottle with water, put the lid on and shake it up. You can spruce up pillows, cushions and any blankets that might be in the living room.

45. Clean Pet Stains from Your Living Room Carpet

For this recipe we're going to need a quarter cup of club soda, baking soda, I have to add a spoonful of liquid dishwashing soap, 2 cups of warm water, a small bowl, a dry cloth and a scrub brush with bristles. Sprinkle over the area where the stain is with baking soda and let it sit for about 30 minutes. Next, add club soda and dish soap, add the water in a bowl mix together and DO NOT SUBSTITUTE VINEGAR AND THEN THINK YOU CAN USE DISH DETERGENT THAT HAS BLEACH IN IT. THIS CAN CAUSE A BAD CHEMICAL REACTION, AND YOU DON'T WANT TO USE THAT. Next, blot out the area with your cloth and get it wet. You can use the scrub brush to get the area cleaned vigorously, and then use your towel again to blot the area. Add more club soda if you need to.

46.   Living Room Floor Cleaner

For this recipe, use the juice of a lemon, a damp cloth, a gallon jug with a lid, a small bowl, 1 gallon of water and 1 tablespoon of flax oil or mineral oil. Mix the juice of the lemon with the oil and a little water in the bowl. Transfer this to the gallon jug and shake it up. You can pour a little into a bucket and mop with it.

47.   Antibacterial Wipes

This recipe is for anytime you are in the living room or just for your living spaces as these areas tend to have a lot of activity with friends and family, and you know that you want to constantly clean up after the kids, wipe counters down, wipe down the coffee table and clean up little spills like from juice and soda.

To make these wipes you will need a roll of paper towels, a storage container that the paper towels can fit into and this will be about half the size of a paper towel roll,
foamy hand wash, about 2 tablespoons, a few drops of lemon essential oil,
a few drops of honor guard protective blend, and a few tablespoons of coconut oil, and
2 cups of warm water. If you really want to make this in a homemade version, you can cut the paper towel roll in half so that is about the size of the toilet paper roll, set it aside and combine the coconut oil and your lemon oil with the honor guard and hand wash in a small mixing bowl.

Take your paper towel roll once it's cut—again, it's going to look like a toilet paper roll, and it might look chewed up on one end depending on how you cut it. Put that end in the bottom of the container that you're going to actually store it in. Then take the 2 cups of water and combine that with the ingredients that you've already mixed and after you mixed it together, actually pour that over the paper towels, which is going to saturate them completely and that's what you want. As it gets wet, wait about 10 minutes and then take the cardboard center out and leave the wipes there. You can use the wipes that you made randomly as you need them, and they will stay wet as long as you keep the lid on. You can use the wipes to wipe down the door knobs, light switches and even things like surface areas where the kids might get hands and fingerprints all over everything.

48. Lavender Scented or Lemon Scented Antibacterial Wipes

    Use the recipe that you have for your antibacterial wipes and substitute your lemon essence essential oil with lavender essential oil, or you can use eucalyptus. If you prefer something like a rose scent, you can use rosehip essential oil as well.

49. Antibacterial Wipes using Baby Wipes:

    To use this version, you're going to actually use the baby wipes container that you may have had and use the wipes that are there. Your ingredients will be one and a half cups of warm water, a few drops of lavender essential oil, a few drops of lemon essential oil, 1 teaspoon of rubbing alcohol and 1 tablespoon of coconut oil. Mix your ingredients together and pour that into the container where the wipes are. You can leave this mixture in there and just remember to drain each wipe as you take it out to use it.

50. Antibacterial Wipes For the Living Room and Living Spaces or Common Areas Using Napkins

    Follow the same recipe as above but instead of using baby wipes, use an old container that you used for baby wipes and when they run out, fill it with napkins. The only problem with this is that when the napkins are saturated, you may find that they tend to fall apart unless they are a thicker consistency like a dinner napkin.

Recipes for Floors

Whether you have tiles that need to be wiped down or you have hardwood floors, the goal with going green and making your own cleaner is to use all natural products and you will find that these Do it Yourself recipes are easy and will have the floors smelling great!

Ingredients will include lemons, water, flax oil, olive oil, or mineral oil. Your equipment will include a mop, bucket, mixing bowl, measuring cups and measuring spoons. You may also want to use a dry or damp cloth to wipe up any messes from the mixing!

51. Wood Floor Cleaner

> You will need lemon juice or squeeze the juice from a lemon, a bucket filled with water, a mop, 1 tablespoon of flax oil, olive oil or mineral oil. Mix the juice of the lemon with the oil and then you can add it to the water. Use your mop and you can clean up all of your wood floors. You can add a little more oil for wood floors but don't make it too much. You're just cleaning them, and you don't want to slip!

52. Tile Floor Cleaner

Fill a large bucket with hot water and add in ½ cup of baking soda. Use your mop to rinse it around and you can mop the floor with this.

53. Cleaning Grease from the Floor

To accomplish this, you can use a little baking soda and sprinkle it on the stain. Next, use a scrub brush to wipe it and a damp cloth to clean up any excess.

54. Clean Stains from Your Carpet

You can start with club soda and a few damp cloths that you soak in the club soda and try to *lift* the stain from the carpet by allowing it to be absorbed in the cloths.

55. Clean Stubborn Stains from Your Carpet

This is similar to the above recipe, but you're going to add a little baking soda to the stain once the club soda is on and scrub it with a scrub brush to get the stain out. DO NOT ADD VINEGAR. Some people use this as a substitute for club soda, but it can act like bleach and discolor your rug. Just add the baking soda and even a few drops of dish soap. MAKE SURE YOUR DISH SOAP DOESN'T HAVE BLEACH IN IT, and you can scrub a stain out. Apply more club soda if needed to saturate the rug.

56. Clean Scented Floors

If you just want to touch up a room and make it smell fresh, use ½ bucket of water and add a few drops of essential oil in the scent that you would like. It can be rose, lemon, vanilla, mint or lavender. Wipe the floor down and let it dry with the new fresh scent!

57. Clean Scented Swiffer Wipes

   Use a few drops of your favorite essential oil on a handy wipe or Swiffer wipe that you would use to dust your floor. Soak it lightly in water to get it wet and then add it to your Swiffer mop. You can use a spray bottle with water if you find that it starts to get dry. This is great if you want to spruce up a room quickly and don't want to deal with a mop.

58. Cleaning Scuff Marks Out of Wood Floors

   Use the inside of a walnut where the actual meat is (the part you eat) and you can use it to rub out a scuff mark on the floor.

59. Other Ways to Clan Scuff Marks Out of Wood Floors

   If you find black scuff marks from the heel of a shoe, you can try using the ball of the shoe and rubbing over the space. Sometimes this loosens up the mark and it will quickly come clean.

60. Antibacterial Cleanser for Dog Mishaps

   You can spray vinegar on the floor to help saturate the area and then wipe it clean with a paper towel.

We know that ensuring that your children have a safe and clean play area is very important, and it's just as important to ensure that you can keep their spaces clean without using toxic chemicals. Use these recipes that you can make in an instant and some that don't even need mixing that are safe, easy and you can share them with friends and family!

Ingredients will include vinegar, various types of essential oils, baking soda, dish soap, and water. Equipment will include things like a blow dryer, measuring cups, measuring spoons, a mixing bowl, spray bottles, labels and a mop and bucket—not that kids are ever messy!

61. Getting Crayon Marks Off of Walls

    This is one of the easiest recipes. Plug in a blow dryer and turn it on. Let the hot air blow over the crayon and you can wipe it off with a cloth. Add a little dish soap to the cloth and moisten it if you see it run but not come completely out.

62. Generic All Purpose Cleaner

For this recipe, you are going to use two cups of water, a quarter cup of lemon juice and 1 cup of hydrogen peroxide. You can mix these in a spray bottle and use it as soon as you need them to help wipe down things like walls, table tops, and areas where the children play.

63. All Purpose Cleaner with Lemon Essential Oil

Some people find that using lemon juice does not last long, and one way to substitute this is to use two cups of water cup of hydrogen peroxide and actual lemon essential oil when you add a few drops as needed to your mixture and put that in your spray bottle.

64. All Purpose Cleaner With Vinegar

Some people find that they think that hydrogen peroxide make block up their spray bottles. An alternative, depending on type of bottle that you have, is to just use vinegar and water where you add a tablespoon of vinegar to a spray bottle full of water and you mix it up and use this on countertops, walls and even floors.

65. How to Scrub Out Grime or Food Stains in a Play Room

If you find that you have areas that are stubborn, you can use baking soda that you apply to a particular spot on your counter or table in the playroom and then take a scrub brush and vigorously rub in that area to get the stain out.

65. Basic Cleaner for a Play Room Mat

For this recipe, you're going to use distilled water, a few drops of lavender oil peppermint oil or tea tree oil. It can be a combination or you can pick your favorite oil. In a spray bottle, mix the water and oil together, and you can spray your children's mats down. If it's grimy, let the water sit for a little while and then wipe it down with a dry cloth.

66. Antibacterial Cleaner for a Play Room Mat

With this recipe, you're going to use a 1:3 ratio water to white vinegar and a few drops of eucalyptus, lavender oil, mint oil or tea tree oil. So in essence to make this recipe, you can take one cup of water, and use 3 cups of white vinegar. You could also use a 50:50 ratio and that can work just as well.

67. Cleaner for Play Areas and Mats

With this particular recipe, you can use Dr. Bronner's soap where you add a few drops to a spray bottle filled with water. You can also add in a little tea tree oil, eucalyptus oil or mint essential oil. Shake it and you can use it in the spray and just wipe down any areas that you find that need to be cleaned.

68. How to Get Paint Off of Children's Hands

One way to quickly get paint off of a child's hand is to rub their hands with olive oil and let it sink in for about 5 to 10 minutes and then you can thoroughly wash their hands with soap. After that, the paint should come out.

69. How to Get Rid of Stains on the Children's Desk and Furniture

You can actually rub a little olive oil into the wood with a dry cloth, and you should be able to rub the marks out.

70. Getting Stains Out of a Carpet in the Playroom

Club soda works well for most stains, but you may have to really soak it in to ensure the stain gets out. Don't be afraid to use a lot of club soda and completely soak a dry cloth then apply it to the area. You want all the stain to be absorbed in the cloth. The stain should come out fine, but you may have to douse it a few times.

Recipes for the Garden

As you get out in your garden, there are few great tips that you can use to help to ensure that you have different types of organic compost, for example, as well as bug repellents and other items that you can make yourself. The ingredients will include products like essential oils, witch hazel, almond oil, water and other ingredients. Your equipment will include things like measuring spoons and measuring cups, a mixing spoon, empty spray bottles and labels to identify what you have in each bottle.

71. Insect Repellent That's all Natural

   Combine 2 tablespoons of witch hazel with 2 tablespoons of grape seed oil or almond oil, and if you can find it, use Neem oil, which is a natural insecticide. You will also need several drops of essential oils. Combine your ingredients into a small spray bottle and shake them together. You can add the essential oils last. Add as much as you want in terms of how strong you want the smell to be.

   To use this type of bug spray, you're going to have to apply it every few hours to keep it handy, and if you want double up your recipe that way you can have to spray bottles for your family. Be sure to label this, and MAKE SURE THAT YOU DON'T USE IT IF YOUR PREGNANT OR NURSING, AND YOU

ARE CAREFUL TO KEEP YOUR PRODUCTS THAT YOU CREATE SAFE AND AWAY FROM CHILDREN.

Another way to make your bug repellent is to change the essential oil as there are different types of oils that repel bugs such as citronella, eucalyptus, bergamot, lemon, peppermint, and tea tree. You can use a combination of these as your essential oils, and you may add anywhere from 50 to a hundred drops total.

73.　Compost Tea Fertilizer

You can make your own fertilizer using about a five gallon bucket of finished compost, and you fill it with water. Let the mixture sit for a couple days and then mix it again as much as you can. As you strain it through a cheese cloth, you can transfer it into another bucket and use the compost in your garden and put that in your compost bin. Then dilute it with water and it should be about a 10 to 1 ratio of water. You can fertilize the soil with this or use a spray bottle and spray the leaves.

74.　Grass Fertilizer

To make this, save grass clippings from your lawn and fill it in a five gallon bucket about three quarters of the way fall and then add water so it is just a few inches from the top. Let it sit for a couple of days and make sure to check it at least once a day. Strain the excess liquid off and dilute it with equal parts water. This will serve as your fertilizer for your plants or you can use spray bottle and put on your leaves.

75.　Vinegar Fertilizer

This is a way that you can help your plants to grow using household fertilizer. Use one tablespoon of white vinegar in a gallon of water and use it to water your plants. You can update this about every 3 or 4 months.

76. Natural Weed Killer

In a large pan, you want to boil about four quarts of distilled vinegar. Once it comes to a boil, remove it from the heat. The fumes might be a little unpleasant, but they are harmless. Add 1 cup of salt while it's still hot and stir it in. Then you are going to add about a tablespoon of dish detergent. MAKE SURE THAT THE DISH DETERGENT DOES NOT HAVE BLEACH IN IT. THIS CAN CAUSE A BAD REACTION.

You are going to use this mixture through a spray bottle to kill your weeds. This is a very strong and potent solution. Don't let it get on to your plants but only on the weeds. If you spray the weeds, don't spray your plants and don't let the water get so saturated that it could spill over into your plants roots. This is weed killer, you can keep this separately in the garage. MAKE SURE ITS LABELED AND THAT IT'S SEALED TIGHTLY. It's not toxic, but it can irritate the eyes in the skin. IT'S JUST VERY PUNGENT SO BE SURE TO KEEP IT AWAY FROM CHILDREN.

77. For Natural Plant Food, Try This Recipe

Combine together a tablespoon of Epsom salt, a teaspoon of salt, a teaspoon of baking powder and a half teaspoon of household ammonia into a one gallon container of water. You can water plants with this about once a month. This can help your tomatoes, trees, and even roses to grow.

78. A Simple Version of Plant Food

You can add just two teaspoons of Epsom salt, and this can help your plants. Read the side of Epsom salt bottle for further directions.

Another alternative is to use leftover cold coffee, and this you can sprinkle on to plants as well.

80.   Another method for helping your plants is to add egg water to them

The way to do this is to save eggshells, as much as you can. After about a month, let your eggshells build up into a glass jar. Keep adding eggshells and maybe after a month or so, once the eggshells are filled up as much as possible in the jar, you can add water to it and put in about a gallon of plain water to 1 cup of eggshells. Use the water to water your plants. You can also use this recipe with coffee grinds, eggshells and a little bit of Epsom salt. Mix it together and spoon it into the flowering plants, and this can help if you have something like African violets.

Recipes for the Garage and Car

If you're working in your garage or car, we know there are a lot of areas where you can use Do it Yourself recipes for wipes, cleaners and other areas. Because you want to keep these spaces safe, clean and organized, try a few of these recipes to help you in the garage and with your car!

81. Antibacterial Wipes for Your Car

    For this recipe, you will need an old container that you would have baby wipes in or a wipe dispenser, 1 cup of water, 2 tablespoons of ammonia, 2 tablespoons of dish soap (DO NOT USE A BLEACH VERSION—we recommend Dawn), and ¼ cup of rubbing alcohol. For this recipe, you're going to mix all of your ingredients in a mixing bowl, and you can then pour it over dinner napkins, paper towels, or cloths that you make yourself. Cover the container and use them as you need to. If you make the cloth version, you can put these in the hamper and wash with the regular laundry when you're ready to throw in a load.

82. Cloth wipes for Your Antibacterial Container

    Take old t-shirts, preferably baby t-shirts which are smaller and lighter, cut them into squares that you can use as individual wipes.

83. Antibacterial Container

   To make your own antibacterial containers, make sure to save old dispensers with the lids and you can recycle these. For example, you can use baby wipe containers, old Clorox wipe containers or Lysol wipe containers. Just rinse them clean, and they are ready to use!

84. Car Wipes Using Old Socks

   Take a sock that you no longer need. It doesn't matter if it has a match or not, and you can use this to wipe the car down. One sock can be adding wax to the car, and one can be taking it off and buffing it.

85. Garage Room Floor Cleaner

   To keep your floors tidy and free from lint, add 1/8 cup of baking soda to 1/2 gallon of water that you fill a bucket with. You can then mop the floor with it, or use a sponge and clean around the common areas, near the car, bikes, etc.

86. Homemade Spray for Grease Stains

   Because the garage usually will have grease in it, you may find clothes with grease on them or spots that you can't degrease easily. Try this recipe: 1 cup of warm water, 3 tablespoons of baking soda, 1/3 cup of ammonia, 1/3 cup of Dawn or Palmolive dish detergent. Mix the ingredients and pour them into a spray bottle. Shake the bottle well. You can then apply it to grease spots or any laundry that gets grease on it from the car or garage. DO NOT ADD ANY BLEACH PRODUCT TO THIS RECIPE AS IT HAS AMMONIA. THIS CAN CAUSE A BAD REACTION.

87. Homemade Spray for Grass Stains in the Garage

If you find clothing with grass stains, or areas where the grass clippings have stained the garage floor, you can use the spray you just made and apply it. Just let it sit for a few minutes and wipe it up. DO NOT ADD ANY BLEACH PRODUCT TO THIS RECIPE AS IT HAS AMMONIA. THIS CAN CAUSE A BAD REACTION.

88. Homemade Car Wax

Ingredients will include 1 tablespoon pine oil, 16 ounces of turpentine, 2 tablespoons of beeswax (yellow) and 8 ounces of Carnauba wax. This recipe can help to wax one standard-size car. Test a small area before applying. Using a double boiler, you can heat the Carnauba wax and the beeswax, then stir and let it cool until it's almost solid. Next, add in the pine oil and the turpentine. When you're ready to use it, take a rag and dip it in, and you can apply it.

89. Car Waxing Cloths

Cut up old t-shirts that have no rhinestones or coloring on them, and you can make them into large solid squares. Keep them on the side for waxing the car and another pile for taking off wax or cleaning up spills!

90. Homemade Car Washing Mix
For this easy recipe, you will need a bucket of warm water and a few drops of liquid castile soap. Add a few drops to the bucket as you add water and you can start washing the car!

Recipes for Outdoor Spaces

When you think about outdoor spaces, of course you want to barbeque, enjoy the deck, the balcony or backyard. We have a few great recipes to fight off the bugs and mosquitoes and ensure you can enjoy your outdoor space! Ingredients will include various essential oils, candle wax and wicks, while supplies will include glass containers for your candles and spray bottles for your various sprays.

91. Citronella Candles

 You will need clear glass jars, wicks, wax and citronella essential oil. Take your glass jars and fill them with one wick each. You can stick the wicks to the bottom with tape or hot glue. Set the glass jars in the oven to heat them gently at the lowest temperature. This will help the wax to cool evenly. Wear gloves so you don't burn yourself. If you use flaky wax, it will reduce to about half the size. Use a double boiler and add the wax into the top. The liquid will start to separate when you boil the water in the bottom. You will see it pull away from the actual wax. Add about 3 drops of citronella oil for each cup of wax; mix it in. Pour the wax gently into your jars. As you will have gloves on, try to do this over the sink to avoid any spills. Fill the jars and cut the excess wicks when the jars are cool to the touch. When you're ready to use them, spread them out around your backyard but not where children are playing or where the dog is running!

92. Eucalyptus Candles

 Use the recipe above and you can add eucalyptus essential oil. A good idea is to make all three and have an insect free zone for hours—that will smell heavenly! It might also smell like barbeque once you get the food on the grill!

93. Mint Candles

    Use the candle recipe and add peppermint essential oil. Keep in mind if you make several candles at once, you'll have enough to last you all summer long!

94. Instant Bug Repellent

    Mix together in a small bowl essential oils that include eucalyptus, peppermint, patchouli, citronella, and lemongrass. Depending on how much you mix together, you will have a strong repellent against bugs, ants, flees and mosquitoes. Dilute with water and add to a spray bottle to apply. Never add straight essential oil to the skin. It's too harsh. Reapply every few hours and do skin checks to ensure you have no allergies to any of the oils.

95. Natural Bug Spray

    Mix 2 tablespoons of witch hazel with 2 tablespoons of grape seed oil or almond oil, and several drops of essential oil. Combine your items into a spray bottle and shake them up. Apply every few hours. Do not use if you are pregnant or nursing. Make sure to label your spray.

96. Bug Repellent

    Use essential oils that repel bugs like citronella, eucalyptus, bergamot, lemon, peppermint and tea tree oils. Mix together 50 – 100 drops and add to water in a spray bottle. Test it on your skin first to ensure you have no allergies.

97. Bug Spray for Kids

Make your essential oil and add it to a spray bottle with warm water, shake it up. Use a test area on your child and apply it there to make sure they don't have an allergic reaction.

98. Bug Spray for Dogs

    Apply a few drops of citronella essential oil that you have diluted with water to the back of your dog's neck. Check with your veterinarian to ensure your dog is the right size and doesn't have a reaction before applying.

99. Bug Spray for Dogs

    Mix citronella oil and cedar oil together, just a few drops, dilute it in a spray bottle with water. You can lightly mist the back of your dog, do not get it near their eyes or mouth and make sure to wipe off the excess. Also make sure they don't lick the spray. If they start to, do not use it. Check with your veterinarian before applying.

100. Citronella Spray

    If you are traveling and want to make a fun way to ward off bugs, add 50 – 100 drops of citronella essential oil to a spray bottle filled with water and mix it up. You can spray the area where you are eating in the back yard to ward off bugs.

Conclusion

We hope you enjoyed your Do it Yourself home cleaning recipes. These are products that we use anytime you need them, and they are safe to use and not harmful to you, your family, pets or the environment. That's why we tried to give you an assortment of recipes that you can use to help ensure that as you go green, and as you learn to create your own cleaning products and different sprays, you have a few top choices and you can mix and match the oils to scent the products.

Not only will this help you to make your home a more natural environment, but it will be one that is safer and you don't have to breathe in toxic, cancer-causing chemicals. These are actually products you can touch and breathe in as they are not harmful to you or your skin. That's why we wanted to create this book of easy recipes for you to enjoy and we hope that you found it useful and it not only brightens up your home but changes your life!

References

http://www.mnn.com/your-home/at-home/stories/how-to-clean-an-oven-naturally

http://www.apartmenttherapy.com/20-diy-green-cleaning-recipes-141129

http://www.apartmenttherapy.com/how-to-make-your-own-bathroom-cleaners-shopping-list-recipes-108150

http://www.diynatural.com/homemade-laundry-detergent-soap/

http://www.diynatural.com/category/cleaning/

http://www.diynatural.com/homemade-fabric-softener-dryer-sheets/

http://www.apartmenttherapy.com/how-to-make-your-own-wood-poli-138622

http://www.apartmenttherapy.com/how-to-make-your-own-clothing-98404

http://www.apartmenttherapy.com/how-to-clean-food-pet-stains-f-109578

http://doterrablog.com/diy-homemade-disinfecting-wipes/

http://www.onegoodthingbyjillee.com/2012/08/make-your-own-swipes-sanitizing-wipes.html

http://housekeeping.about.com/od/surfaceswalls/tp/crayonwalls.htm

http://www.apartmenttherapy.com/an-excellent-homemade-threeing-116677

http://www.apartmenttherapy.com/6-ways-to-clean-with-olive-oil-117261

http://www.diynatural.com/homemade-insect-mosquito-repellent/

http://www.doityourself.com/stry/homemade-weed-killer-recipe

http://www.creativehomemaking.com/garden/homemade-plant-food.shtml

http://www.onegoodthingbyjillee.com/category/life

http://www.onegoodthingbyjillee.com/2011/08/giving-bounce-dryer-sheets-bounce.html

http://www.onegoodthingbyjillee.com/2011/08/shout-it-out-homemade-version.html
http://www.makeyourown.net/car_wax.shtml

http://frugalliving.about.com/od/affordabletransportation/tp/Car_Cleaner_Recipes.htm

http://blog.diynetwork.com/maderemade/how-to/bug-off-make-your-own-citronella-candles/